All Mart

All Mart

By

L.T. Willis

Editor
Ray Glandon

Senior Publisher
Steven Lawrence Hill Sr.

Awarded Publishing House
ASA Publishing Company
Established Since 2005

ASA Publishing Company
Nominated for 2012 Better Business Bureau Torch Award
105 E. Front St., Suite 201A, Monroe, Michigan 48161
www.asapublishingcompany.com

Copyrights©2012 L.T. Willis, All Rights Reserved
Book: All Mart
Date Published: 12.11.12
Edition: 1 *Trade Paperback*
Book ASAPCID: 2380618
ISBN: 978-1-886528-50-5
Library of Congress Cataloging-in-Publication Data

This book was published in the United States of America.
State of Michigan

A Publisher Trademark Title page

Table of Contents

All Mart

All Mart

By

L.T. Willis

Acknowledgements

I am thankful to God for trusting me as one of His vessels. Without Him, I completely understand that I'm just existing and not living! I'm grateful to my wife, Kimberly, for being a wonder-woman! You've been a true help-meet! You've helped me meet deadlines. You've helped me reach my potential. I'm grateful to my children for being my inspiration! I'm grateful for my parents, Pastor Arthur C. Willis, Sr. and Janice Willis for training me in the way of God. I'm very thankful to my brothers and sisters for supporting me in ways they don't even realize. I'm thankful for my brothers in ministry, Rev. Kenneth Pierce II, Rev. Terrance L. Johnson, and Pastor David A. Johnson II. To the Pentecost Missionary Baptist Church, thank God for you and your support. To the Concerned Council of Baptist Pastors and Ministers of Detroit and Vicinity, thank God for you and your support. I'm grateful to a long list of family, friends, and co-laborers of the Christian faith- Pastors and Ministers from around the country. To my editor, Ray Glandon, I thank God for you and your kindness. Your knowledge has helped me grow not only as a writer but also as a person. May God bless you tremendously for the work you've done. Lastly, to Steven Hill, Sr. and the ASA Publishing family, thank you for your creativeness and your professionalism.

A S A   P u b l i s h i n g   C o m p a n y

Foreword

THERE ARE MANY THINGS THAT COULD BE SAID ABOUT the author of this book. He is an emerging voice in the kingdom, a husband, a father, a pastor's son, a preacher, a writer, a leader, and a servant. Since he stepped into an arena where men of his age are rarely acknowledged, he has neither apologized for his passion nor acquiesced to the naysayers. Instead, he has chosen to embark upon a path of humility as he seeks to make a mark on his generation that will never be erased.

To be sure, his humble spirit and biblical prowess are earning him respect even amongst those who are just being introduced to his amazing gifts. I believe that this book unveils his creativity and a relevance that every person who reads it may gain from its insight. As he releases more and more of his intrinsic gift, I watch with great appreciation as he not only blossoms himself but also helps others to unlock, unmask, and unearth the hidden treasure they were often oblivious to before encountering his ministry.

I have known LT Willis and his family for many years. I met him in my adolescence when his father, Pastor Arthur C. Willis, Sr., was a Deacon at the Greater Middle Missionary Baptist Church. His father is now a premiere pastor in the Metropolitan Detroit area, and the mantle has now fallen on the son. Generational mantles are often unavoidable when the distinctions of gift are unique and the assignments are God-ordained. This generational line is no different. To be sure about it, LT walks in the footsteps of a powerful lineage and legacy, and God has positioned him with poise to make a lasting impact in his era.

I have watched him grow from being a skilled musician and passionate young preacher to a mature scholar and spiritual technician of the word of God. Having observed him up close, I can attest that his humility is persuasive. The respect he has earned has offered opportunities for his gifts to be heard amongst great men. I was delighted to learn that he had decided to share his ideology for this compilation of writing and the masterful illustrations that he extracts straight from the scriptures. This book will help those who read it to "Save a Life, and Live Better."

As I mentioned before, I have observed him as a son, a husband, a father, a student of scripture. Now, I am witness to him as a preacher of the gospel. In each of these areas, he continues to produce a fruitful, purposeful, and meaningful life. It is my hope that as you travel down each aisle in this book that you will place in your basket the necessities of life that will become treasures of enhancement for you. In doing so, you will be able to give from your own basket of treasure and share it with all whom you encounter as generously as he has shared in the pages of this work with you. If you believe, as I do, what the Apostle Paul declared in the book of Ephesians that the exceeding riches of His inheritance are hidden in His people, you will want those riches to be identified in your own life, and you will want to discover the great extent God has gone through so that you may enjoy His awesome abundance. This is a navigation escort filled with Scriptural insights that will transform you into a bargain shopper and usher you into a richer fuller expression of yourself on earth. I am sure that you will benefit from your time spent reading this book and be transformed from the dismal into the delightful, from the tranquil to the transformational, to the fulfilled individual you were created to be. To those of you who have not met him, I am humbled and honored to be a forerunner to prepare your heart for the dynamic and thought-provoking ministry of Reverend LT Willis.

Pastor David Allan Johnson, II
DAJ2 Ministries, Detroit, MI

ASA Publishing Company

A S A Publishing Company

About the Book

This book is easy to read and simple to understand; that's what makes it exciting to read. It is one that you will want to keep in your library because it is filled with wisdom. You can see that the Holy Spirit has taken control of LaThomas' pen. Like his first book, *The Way Out is … Through: God is with you in your wilderness experience,* this book is extraordinary! I am delighted and excited in what the Lord is doing with LaThomas through his writing. I know that you will be blessed after reading it.

-Rev. Dr. Arthur C. Willis Sr., Senior Pastor
Pentecost Missionary Baptist Church, Romulus, MI

When LT informed me he was writing another book, I was extremely excited. When you read his work, you will notice there is always something that will jump off the pages and push or encourage the readers to make it another day. As I've read LT's work, I found it very inspiring. This book, "All-Mart," is a book you will not be able to put down. As you read, I want to encourage you to think about those moments you've been making your grocery/shopping list at home for all your daily essential needs. Let your mind focus on the needs and wants of that grocery list.

Before reading sit down, get a pen and paper, and write down your list for "All Mart," the one-stop shop for all your essential spiritual and encouragement needs. At "All Mart," you will find all types of fruit to keep you spiritually healthy (Galatians 5: 22-23), everything you need to live a better spiritual life. At "All Mart," your one-stop shop, you will be inspired and given insight on how to deal with the daily tests and trials that life can bring your way. This author has a true and scriptural understanding of those. So enjoy and be encouraged. Remember, "We are living this life just to live again, so make it count."

-Rev. Kenneth C. Pierce, II, Youth Pastor
Beulah Missionary Baptist Church, Westland, MI

When Rev. LT Willis asked me if I would consider writing about his book, there was no way I would have refused. LT is someone that I consider to be a brother, and it has been awesome to witness how GOD has propelled LT's ministry over the past few years. Now we are at the next phase in his ministry as an author and in the words of my pastor, Dr. Robert E. Starghill, Sr., "GOD has done it again." He has used LT to write another book that will challenge and encourage us. Just from reading the title, All-Mart, it ministers and let's us know that everything that we need is in Christ. It amazes me the time we spend searching for what we feel that we need spiritually and emotionally. Now we have a reminder like *All-Mart* to tell us to stop wasting our time and energy searching and to start seeking. *All-Mart* reminds us what JESUS told us in

Matthew 6:33, that everything we need will be supplied if we would just seek the Kingdom of GOD. So, my brothers and sisters, you began this new spiritual adventure in this book. Now open your hearts and minds to what the LORD is saying through Rev. Willis and get ready for your spiritual shopping spree where everything that you are ready to purchase has already been paid for back on Calvary.

-Rev. Terrance L. Johnson, Minister of Youth
Samaritan Missionary Baptist Church, Detroit, Mi.

A S A   P u b l i s h i n g   C o m p a n y

Introduction

      As a child, I hated shopping! I absolutely hated it! It wasn't so much that I didn't like getting new things or wearing nice clothes. It wasn't that I didn't like my family to have nice things. I hated shopping as a child because my mother, fashionable as she was, would always take hours shopping. Being the youngest child, I always had to go with her when she went shopping. Of all the stores we went to, the one that I dreaded me the most was Winkleman's Clothing Store. Winkleman's was a clothing store for women in the early 1990s. I literally came to tears each time we stopped in this store because I knew it wasn't going to be a pit stop. Nothing against the store or my mother, but the store was not for me! There were mannequins everywhere, and it appeared as though I was trapped in my mother's closet! Now that I think about it, my father never came with us. He was smart, and I had a lot to learn. As I look back now, my mother would take "all day" shopping because if she was going to invest her money in something, she wanted to make sure it looked right, felt right, and had the right price. This may be the reason for lengthy shopping for some people. However, whether the shopping spree is long or short, most people just want to make sure they get their money's worth. You may be thinking that the nature of gender shopping shows that women take longer to shop than men. Whatever the case may be, men and women both shop. Whether it's at Macy's or Home Depot, they shop!

I define shopping as browsing through select items that best meet one's social, mental, physical, and spiritual desires with the possibility of purchasing said item(s). In the past, shopping was time consuming for most consumers. If one store didn't have what you needed , you had to drive across town to get to another, perhaps stopping to get something to eat, getting gas, and wasting half your day. Soon the obvious question was asked. Why couldn't food and household goods be in the same store? Why couldn't toiletries and sporting goods be in one store? Why couldn't a restaurant and a bank be in the same place? Well, several years ago Sam Walton and his brother, Bud Walton, made it possible. They founded the superstore, Wal-Mart. Wal-Mart was your one-stop-shop for living your life. Wal-Mart appeals to all three social classes: lower, middle, and upper class. Wal-Mart literally has everything that one needs to live.

Here lies my point: Neither Wal-Mart nor any other Mart has everything you need to live eternally, except … "All-Mart," the spiritual superstore. All-Mart is simply a paradigm of what Jesus explains in Luke 11:9-10 which says:

"So I say to you, ask, and it will be given to you; seek , and you will find; knock, and it will be opened to you. (10) For everyone who asks receives, and he who seeks finds, and to him who knocks it will be opened.   -NKJV

Allow your mind to travel with mine as we shop through an imaginary building, a realistic marketplace for your spiritual growth in the Christian faith. While All-Mart is not a building, it is a place. It's a place of spiritual consciousness. The items on your shopping list may be gathered by way of worship services, bible study, and personal prayer to God, who is our Father in heaven. Our homes are furnished and our refrigerators are full. But at some point, we must replace what we've run out of or worn down.

A "mart" is defined as a trading place where goods are sold. I must issue this disclaimer that the church itself is not a trading place, which angered Jesus in John 2:13-16.

(13) Now the Passover of the Jews was at hand, and Jesus went up to Jerusalem. (14) And He found in the temple those who sold oxen and sheep and doves, and the money changers doing business. (15) When He had made a whip of cords, He drove them all out of the temple, with the sheep and the oxen, and poured out the changers' money and overturned the tables. (16) And He said to those who sold doves, "Take these things away! Do not make My Father's house a house of merchandise!"
NKJV

However, society itself can be this trading place because the shelves of life are stocked both with junk food and nutritional food, and if you choose to buy what the devil is selling, your life will be a living hell. When an individual goes to shop at any mart, market, or mall, it is to restock, restore, or to redeem. In other words, they're going to get something that they need for everyday maintenance of self or possessions. Beloved, I say to you, the same is said within the body of Christ. Circumstances and situations arise in our lives, sometimes without notice, and we run out of or don't have the things that we need to maintain. How many people have you met that have lost hope or have become burdened with life's troubles because they don't have what they need to make it in life? Most of us at some point or another begin to lose our way because our spiritual drawers, closets, and rooms are not filled with the things we need to be the best people that we can be. The fact is nearly everything that we shop for is for the benefit of us or our family. Whether it's clothes, accessories, paint, media, food, or air conditioning, they are all purchased to help us maintain a lifestyle that we desire. If we are missing any of these things or are running low, we make a list and shop for what we need. Thank God that Christ has made it so in our life.

Beloved, if you find yourself struggling to maintain in a perilous world, make a list and let's go shopping. I'll be your kingdom-agent. Be careful of what you put in your basket. Please understand that your shopping cart or basket is an extension of self. In other words, it's your property! It belongs to you! Whatever you put in your basket is going home with you. When grocery shopping, it is important to consider the nutritional value of each food. Hebrews 12:1 says:

Therefore we also, since we are surrounded by so great a cloud of witnesses, let us lay aside every weight, and the sin which so easily ensnares us, and let us run with endurance the race that is set before us,

-NKJV

Beloved, some things you just don't need! On the other hand, you may need to get enough items to share with others. As my kids say, "sharing is caring!" When my wife goes grocery shopping, she'll purchase food items that stretch, so our family and visitors can be fed adequately. While at All-Mart, I encourage you to embrace this same mentality! Purchase those items that can stretch because when you stretch, you reach others easier! And finally, be sure to sign up for the savings card because you'll need that to verify that you are a member of the body of Christ. With one scan, everything that you have in your basket has already been paid for at Mt. Calvary by the death, burial, and resurrection of Jesus Christ. Enjoy your shopping spree! Save a life, and live better!

A S A P u b l i s h i n g C o m p a n y

Kiosk: Bank of Life
Matthew 16:24

Here to the right you'll find one of our many kiosks. A bank is a place of necessity for most people! The bank has made saving and spending convenient in the 21st century. Many of us have access to banking from computers and cell phones. However, it is still necessary to have banks available for people to walk in and get customer service. One primary goal of a bank is to assure customers are satisfied and comfortable as they manage their money. This goal would be difficult to meet without the member depositing their money in the bank. Understand that where you deposit money, you certainly can withdraw it. Beloved, the same concept works in the kingdom of God. Deposit your life, and you can withdraw life in Christ. Christ explains in Matthew 16:24-25:

Then Jesus said to His disciples,
"If anyone desires to come after Me,
let him deny himself, and take up his cross, and follow Me.
(25) For whoever desires to save his life will lose it, but
whoever loses his life for My sake will find it.
NKJV

One of the most difficult things to do in the body of Christ is to give up your fleshly desires and walk with Christ. This is indeed a process that should be defined by progress. In other words, the process of individuals denying themselves and taking up their cross is measured by progression. I must boldly declare that when you are a Christian, life is not about you! You cannot strengthen your faith by being concerned about you! It's all about Jesus.

In 2004, NBC aired a reality TV show entitled "The Biggest Loser." It is aired on NBC in many countries, and it centers on overweight contestants attempting to lose weight for a cash prize. Overweight simply means weight that an individual shouldn't carry. In other words, the contestants on this show are losing to gain. In Matthew 16:24, Jesus begins to tell the disciples about His purpose and sufferings, that He must go to Jerusalem, which is where the sacrifices were offered, and He being the Great Sacrifice, had to go there. Jesus opens His statement with an "if," which implies choice. The second word in this sentence is "anyone," which implies an open invitation. Beloved, banks operate the same way. Anyone can walk in and apply to become a member of that bank as long as they have something to deposit. Jesus says, "anyone," meaning there is no discrimination, bias, prejudice, prestige, or social status required in this invitation. The only requirement is that whoever accepts this invitation must deny themselves. Denial is something that we must remember while shopping here at All-Mart.

Denial is one of the most common defense mechanisms, psychologically speaking. Denial is simply refusing to acknowledge that an event has occurred. The person affected simply acts as if nothing happened, behaving in ways that others may see as bizarre. It may also have a significant conscious element, where the sufferer is simply 'turning a blind eye' to an uncomfortable situation. People take credit for their successes and find good reason for their failures, blaming the situation on other people, etc. Some alcoholics may vigorously deny that they have a problem. Many optimists may deny that things may go wrong. Pessimists may deny success will come. Some people don't have a problem using denial. However, self-denial seems to be a problem when it comes to sacrificing our own desires or interests for a greater good. Perhaps the slogan in this Bank of Life should be, "It's not about you!" Jesus' disciples were unable to grasp this concept that Jesus was explaining, that they would have to suffer. They saw the winds obey Him, they saw Him heal numerous people. Now He's telling them that they will suffer? I could only imagine how they were feeling, and some of you may be able to relate as well. Lord, you have all power, why do I have to suffer? Can't you just stop the bleeding, God? The disciples only thought about dignity and power. But, beloved, consider this statement by Jesus to be that of growing pains.

In verse 22 in Matthew 16, Peter had rebuked Jesus ("not You Lord"). Then in v23 Jesus called Peter the enemy because Peter attempted to stand in God's way by telling Jesus he wouldn't have him to suffer. Understand that anything that stands in God's way is of the enemy. Whether it's family, friends, coworkers, or social networks, if it's in the way of the will of God, it is of the enemy! This is precisely why Jesus rebuked Peter by saying, "Get behind Me, and not depart from Me." Some folks need to be rebuked and reminded where their placement should be, and that's behind Jesus. Too many of us are trying to walk beside Jesus, but Isaiah reminds us that His thoughts are not our thoughts, and His ways are not our ways. Even as the heavens are higher above the earth, so to are His ways and thoughts higher than ours. Our purpose is not be consumed with trying to help God out. He doesn't need our help! To be a disciple of Christ you have to be willing to suffer and lose your life for Him. Paul says in Romans 12 to present your bodies a living sacrifice, holy, acceptable to God, which is your reasonable service. Some haven't denied themselves and have been selling out for the world. Consider losing your life for Christ to be a deposit in which you're able to withdraw the benefits of following Him when you allow Him to manage those things you've deposited to Him.

Aisle 1: Fruits of the Spirit
Galatians 5:22-23

One of the first sections that you pass upon entering a grocery store or superstore is the fruit section. Most kids by-pass this section because they're ready for the junk food, which will be addressed in forthcoming chapters. Fruits are some of those foods we need that help us stay healthy by preventing illnesses, developing strength, and increasing productivity, to some degree. In this Christian walk, we must address the fruits of the Spirit and consider them to be of the same necessity. The Apostle Paul's address to the church at Galatia suggested in Galatians 5:22-23:

> But the fruit of the Spirit is love, joy, peace, longsuffering, kindness, goodness, faithfulness, (23) gentleness, self-control. Against such there is no law.
> NKJV

It is important to understand that the Apostle here is explaining that there is no law against loving others, having joy, being peaceful, longsuffering, being kind, being good, being faithful, being gentle, and maintaining self-control. As apples, oranges, bananas, and grapes are good for the human body, so are love, joy, peace and the other mentioned fruits of the Spirit. Many have often heard the cliché, "the fruit doesn't fall far from the tree." Though such a statement can be used with positive or negative connotations, it is certainly indicative of the Christian's possession of the Holy Spirit. As you travel throughout the fruit section, you'll notice several bins of fruit. You can have as much as you like! The more fruit you have, the more productive you'll be. One of the growing challenges that we face as Christians is the fight within our own desires. Sometimes an apple is not as attractive as a bag of chips, but it's healthier. Let's examine each nutritional fact of the fruits of the Spirit.

Love: A feeling of warm personal attachment or deep affection

Love is something that is often misinterpreted. The real meaning of love should certainly be unconditional. Many confuse love with lust while others equate love with like. Christ gave us the greatest example of love. There's no greater love than that great sacrifice that Jesus gave on Mount Calvary. While He knew no sin, He carried all of our sins to the cross. That's what love is about, moving beyond our feelings to make sure others feel our love. Love is not lust. Most teenagers claim to fall in love when it's actually lust. The old folk would simply refer to it as "their nose is wide-open." Lust is certainly that forbidden fruit that we should avoid. One bite into lust and your whole diet could potentially change. Lust satisfies the moment, but love lives beyond the climax.

There have been so many broken relationships because of an absence of love. People have claimed that they "love" someone, something, or that they "love God," but they support it with "like" behavior. When an individual likes something, at some point they will lose their appetite and move on. But with relationships such as marriage, family, and God, you should never lose your appetite. One of the most profound things that I've noticed is that love cannot be given if the giver doesn't possess it. How can you love a person if you don't have love to give? Ponder that question for a while, and then start filling your bag with love. There's no need to weigh it. You can have as much as you like.

Joy: The emotion of great delight or happiness caused by something exceptionally good or satisfying

We are all just a thought away from joy. There is something internal or external that gives us joy. Whether it is people, money, cars, clothes, jewelry, hobbies, or food, something gives us joy. Whether you are a nonverbal or a verbal person, there is something that makes you smile. Joy is one of those feelings that Christians should always have. However, joy is something that people, even some Christians, give away during unpleasant situations. Joy is something that you cannot lose unless you give it away. All of us have smiled at some point in our life. If you haven't smiled in a while, ask yourself why? After you've thought about that, put this book down and go find a mirror. Don't you know that there are people all over this world that are in a worse season of their life than you are? Your issues won't even compare to theirs. The fact that you're able to read or hear these words provides the reality that you're breathing. Not everyone made it to life today, and since you were blessed to get dressed, that's enough to smile. That's joy!

The reason some people walk around hanging their heads down is because they don't have any joy. They've given it away to the enemy. On the other hand, there are some people who are suffering in some area of their life, but they still can manage a smile on their face. That's because they've understood that their situation didn't give them the joy that they have, so their situation can't take joy away from them. Don't base your joy solely on people or material things because those are capable of disappointing you and can let you down. Consider basing your joy on those internal and external factors that are facts of your existence, such as having the activity of your limbs, breath in your body, a job, or a house to live in. Grab bundles of joy because you'll need it during those difficult times in your life.

Peace: A state of tranquility or quiet

Peace has been defined by many as freedom from mayhem. It's freedom from disruption, disorder, and disarray. It's the calm after a storm. Beloved, Jesus called out for peace in the middle of a storm. He spoke to the winds and waves, and they obeyed His call for peace. The storm ceased at the command of Jesus. How could He do it? It's because He's the Prince of Peace. He's able to delegate peace to each and every one of us. Whatever your situation may be, Christ is able to call for peace to park in the middle of your mess. As sure as He's able to do this, we must be proactive, however, and do our part. It is important to understand what peace can do for you; it is, after all, freedom from mayhem. If you're not free from something, then you are a slave to or a servant to it. You must understand that if you remain connected with dysfunction, then it is difficult to digest peace. Every attempt to digest peace in your life will be vomited by the dysfunction that remains in your system.

You must have an appetite for peace because some people are just comfortable in their dysfunction. For example, have you ever known a woman who continues to date a guy that brings dysfunction to the environment? Or, have you ever known a child to have been reared in a dysfunctional environment and when they are grown, they continue the same living standards? The reason for this is that they have developed a dysfunctional hunger drive, therefore needing dysfunction to satisfy their appetite. Also, it's a matter of habit; its all they've known, and it's difficult to break. Beloved, it is important that you change your diet! It may be a challenge at first, just as most diets are.   However, the more peace you have, the more peaceful you'll be.

Possessing peace does not mean doing things that will bring you peace, per say. I know people who seek marijuana, alcohol, or sex to bring them peace. But please don't get it twisted. When the "high" falls, when the hangover wears off, and when the climax has been reached, the reality of dysfunction continues its presence. It is a time where the saints of God need to have an allergic reaction to dysfunction. Anyone with an allergic reaction will display evidence that they can't handle that which they are consuming. Beloved, when you are allergic to dysfunction, it will show, but more importantly, people will see.

Long-suffering: Patiently enduring wrongs or difficulties

Long-suffering is simply the alternative to anger. Consider it as accommodating the emotions of other people directed toward you. When you accommodate others, you assist them with their needs, which means they are the ones who need help. It's not taking things personally. It's simply viewing the situation. You are the one in control of this issue, and the emotions of the other person needs accommodating. For example, I've stayed in hotels and some have been hospitable enough to accommodate me with water, mints, lotions, or towels. Whatever my mood was, they were apt to provide service for me. They understood that my stay was only for a little while, so the things which they provided me were only to be used by me and not taken over by me. The accommodating is free-willed. If we could completely grasp this concept, many family problems, relationship issues, and marital difficulties would be lessened. Simply tolerate the emotion in your mind and think of ways you might be able to accommodate the emotional needs of others. So, you may be reading this and think, that sounds good and all, but it's easier said than done. While I agree, let's try and compare the fruit of long-suffering to "exercising" to provide a more appealing picture of this idea.

Have you ever taken some days, weeks, months, and for some, even years off from exercising? You may be able to testify that the day after you restart your first day of your workout, your body is sore! As you stick with your schedule, however, the soreness will wear off as your muscles become more tolerable. Furthermore, the more you exercise, the stronger you'll become. As you gain strength, a lesser weight or fewer reps are much more manageable for you. In other words, it's nothing to lift a 5lb dumbbell if you've been curling 25lbs regularly. Being more tolerable, you learn not to sweat the small stuff. The more an alcoholic drinks, the more his tolerance increases, which means the more he will drink to reach that point of a drunken state. The more mess you are exposed to, the more you'll be able to tolerate it. This means when problematic emotions are directed toward you, because of long-suffering, you're more able to tolerate it. How many situations are you cognizant of that could have turned out differently had you or someone else just responded differently or not responded at all? Should you just be a doormat or a trash can and let people walk over you? The point here is that while you've been wondering how you or the next person can be involved in a stressful relationship and not lose your mind, that is a testament of long-suffering. You may need bundles of this. Go ahead, fill your bags with this fruit!

Kindness: the quality of being friendly, generous, and considerate

Another rarely picked fruit! You may know it to be southern hospitality, but it's just good ole' kindness. I can remember visiting my family in Roberta, Georgia, where my father is from, and while driving in the community, everyone waved and spoke. Being from Detroit and riding in Georgia as a kid and seeing people speak to one another across roads and in cars at stoplights, that was big news to me. This sort of behavior is almost extinct in some urban neighborhoods. Pushing racial relations to the side, several reasons exist why people just don't speak to one another. If people can't speak to one another, how can they borrow from one another? There used to be a time when it was common for neighbors to borrow food items such as sugar or salt. But now, it seems many neighbors don't even speak to each another. What we're seeing today is simply a phobia, a fear of or disinterest in being kind. A phobia is simple, irrational fear. In other words, it's simply silly to be fearful of being nice. Many young men fear being nice because it would question their "hood credibility" or "toughness." Have you ever experienced riding down the street and get absolutely mean-mugged as you ride by? Handshakes, head-nods, and thumbs-up are slowly being replaced with stare-downs and head-turns. You'll discover that to gain friends you'll have to show yourself as friendly. Being kind will open doors for you to which you thought you'd never gain access. Being kind may actually put you on the pedestal with Batman, Superman, and Spiderman. Fact is, you never know what another person may be going through, and your kind expression or kind words may be just what the doctor ordered. There are people who are in desperate need of a smile or a kind word, and you could be the person to provide them.

Kindness is that fruit that people don't necessarily hunger for or snack after. However, it can definitely be used to fight off any viruses that conflict with your well being. While others might prefer to use an "eye-for-an-eye" philosophy when they have been wronged, you can overpower your enemies with kindness. This ideology is quite elementary. One of the basic steps that elementary schools teach in bully prevention is not allowing the bully to see the victim react. Same thing applies with using the fruit of kindness in our daily walk. Don't let the enemy make you bitter! Stay kind! If you're kind at heart, consider yourself blessed because the world is not abundant with kindness.

Goodness: The quality of being good

Are people born good or bad? Some may say yes. Some may say no. Some may say it depends on what your definitions are. I'll offer two perspectives on this question. In Romans 5, we learn that by one man's disobedience, many were made sinners. Because of the traumatic episode which takes place in the Garden of Eden, transgression is in our blood.

(13) And the LORD God said to the woman, "What is this you have done?"
The woman said, "The serpent deceived me, and I ate." (14) So the LORD God said to the serpent:
"Because you have done this, You are cursed more than all cattle, And more than every beast of the field; On your belly you shall go, And you shall eat dust All the days of your life. (15) And I will put enmity Between you and the woman, And between your seed and her Seed; He shall bruise your head, And you shall bruise His heel."
(16) To the woman He said: "I will greatly multiply your sorrow and your conception; In pain you shall bring forth children; Your desire shall be for your husband, And he shall rule over you."
(17) Then to Adam He said, "Because you have heeded the voice of your wife, and have eaten from the tree of which I

commanded you, saying, 'You shall not eat of it': "Cursed is
the ground for your sake; In toil you shall eat of it All the days
of your life. (18) Both thorns and thistles it shall bring forth
for you, And you shall eat the herb of the field. (19) In the
sweat of your face you shall eat bread Till you return to the
ground, For out of it you were taken; For dust you are, And to
dust you shall return."
Gen 3:13-19
NKJV

Here we have the biblical perspective. Because of
the transgression of Adam and Eve and being our
first parents, they have passed sin down in our
genes through one blood. The scriptures provide
to us that all have sinned and fallen short of the
glory of God (Romans 3:23); therefore no one is
perfect. But does that mean that people are born
"bad"? Not necessarily! What it means is that we
are born with transgression in our blood. What it
means is that no one can be compared to the
greatness and goodness of Jesus Christ who knew
no sin but took on the sins of many to redeem
those who confess Him as the Risen Savior. This is
the very reason why, in the Christian faith, babies
are christened, people must accept Christ as their
savior and be baptized. In other words, once we
have a physical birth, because of transgression in
our blood, we must have a spiritual rebirth. We
must be born again.

A philosophical perspective would suggest
that because we live by moral standards and
values, which are supported by laws, policies, and
spiritual principals, people are born to be

redirected to compliance. In others words, we don't teach our children how to be "bad." We teach them how to do the right thing. We have to guide them and instruct them how to abide by rules and morals. We don't have to teach them how to be "bad." If we fail to enforce any rules, set standards, or encourage moral living, children will naturally engage in defiance because of ignorance. Are people born "bad"? No, people are not born "bad." People are born to be instructed, to be taught the quality of good. That means being compliant and not defiant to directives. In our case, it is the Word of God. Because God made us in His image (Genesis 1:26), we have a quality of being good! Please feel free to grab a host of the goodness fruit. The more the merrier!

Faithfulness: fidelity, the quality of being faithful

So many relationships are ruined, ruptured, and ripped apart because of infidelity. When we begin to discuss faithfulness, we must discuss faith. Biblically, faith is the substance of things hoped for and the evidence of things unseen. One cannot truly be faithful without knowing what faith is. It is the assurance of something without even seeing it. A husband can know without a doubt that his wife is really out with the girls and not out with a guy or vice versa. While he or she isn't physically there, they have faith that the other is abiding to the vows they shared on their wedding day. This faith is put into action by trust. Where there is little trust, there is little faith. Faithfulness is about being full of faith. Are you full of faith? Can God trust you in your relationship with Him? Can God trust you with the gifts He's given to you? Can God trust you with the assignment that He has for your life? These are all questions only you can answer. But I must address that being faithful is required even in terrible times and trying tribulations.

Sometimes on this path of righteousness, we don't want to behave in righteous ways. Situations arise in our lives where we sometimes literally want to give up on doing what we told God we would do. We sometimes want to bail out on our commitments to Him. Some shift their focus entirely to their troubles, and they lose their faith at that point. We encounter pivotal situations where we have to choose to bail out or stay committed to God. I admire those individuals who have been in relationships where they have been hurt by the other individual, or where circumstances caused a strain on the relationship, but they remained faithful to the commitment. When you remain faithful in a relationship after dismal experiences, the relationship will strengthen! Beloved, be faithful to God! Be faithful to one another! Gather as much of this faithfulness fruit as you can. People have left because things didn't go their way, but they later found out that the grass wasn't any greener on the other side. Be faithful!

Gentleness: Considerate or kindly in disposition; amiable and tender

This is not a very popular fruit. Some describe it as bitter-sweet! Most people tend to skip over this section. So a lot of it gets thrown away because not too many people want to indulge in gentleness. There could be several reasons for this, but I'd offer the main reason to be, it's just not attractable. Whether this attraction is in appearance or taste, people skip over the gentleness fruit. Many times individuals feel as if they have to prove themselves of something, and being tough is the way to prove their realness. Sad to say, but many Christians become so caught up in the misfortunes of life that they forget Christ wants us to be gentle. Now this concept may go over well with some, but not with others. It seems as if the inner city youth have made themselves allergic to this fruit, thus creating a phobia to gentleness, which has spread to suburbia. Young people have so much to give to this society, but some fail to walk in their purpose simply because of the pressures and desires to be rough and tough. Think about it! When was the last time you heard a generation of young people saying "yes ma'am," "yes sir," "no thank you," "excuse me sir," or even "thank you"? These common phrases of respect and kindness are endangered species. When I grew up, my parents instilled in me how to be gentle by being mannerly. As I went through my adolescence, I ventured away from that due to social and peer influences, saying things like, "what," "huh," "yep," which then led to my disposition becoming so unapproachable and rough, that I was labeled by my peers as antisocial. As I entered early adulthood and started to meet people in businesses and other organizations, I soon came to realize that a simple "yes sir" or a kind disposition, such as a smile, could really take you places you never would have imagined. When I look at our society today, I see so many people with frowns on their faces, making them very unapproachable. Don't get me wrong, several variables contribute to the disposition of an individual, whether it's personal, environmental, or familial. However, "you" have the ultimate control of your disposition, which may open closed doors for you.

As Christians, we must remember that the gentle fruit that Apostle Paul is referring to is a suggestive requirement in the body of Christ. If anyone knew about being rough, it was Paul. His conversion from Saul to Paul on that road to Damascus gave him a new outlook on life. He was indeed blinded to restore a new way of seeing things. One perspective was that the body of Christ should be gentle. As we are here in this earthly tabernacle, we are to minister to others. We are here to meet the spiritual and emotional needs of others, simply by our disposition. People have needs and will look to you to meet them if you say you're a child of God. Have you ever had to blow your nose with Hardwound Brown Paper Towel (that stuff in the dispenser at elementary schools)? If not, let me tell you that it is very uncomfortable, especially if you have sinus issues. Kleenex, on the other hand, won't cut you, and it folds nicely. The comparison here is simple. Hardwound Brown Paper Towel comes in greater quantity per package but is rough in use. Kleenex comes in lesser quantity but is soft. Let me tell you, even though you're soft, you're valuable! When you start to care more about your disposition being gentle, then you'll reap the benefits.

Self-Control: controlling your impulses (emotions, desires, behavior)

This is one of those fruits that don't have the best taste. Too sweet for some, too tangy for others! Whatever it may be, many saints are lacking self-control. I will not tell you that self-control is simple. It is actually a very complicated discipline! When it comes to self-control and sin, to reduce those desires or to respond to those desires, it is imperative that the elements of the sin be removed! If you're having a hard time controlling your sexual desires, stop answering the phone in the middle of the night. If you can reduce the desire, you can stop the behavior. Our behavior is simply a response to the desires that we are trying to control. So many believers are impulsive in their journey, and this speaks of spiritual maturity. People who are impulsive often have no regard for the consequences of their actions. Young people, there is absolutely a consequence for every decision that you make, albeit good or bad. The same can be said for those of all ages. However, young people are in a transitioned season of life, and those decisions that they make impulsively, they'll have to live with for the rest of their lives. You'll have to serve the sentence, raise that child out of wedlock, or have that condition for a season in your life when you could've been doing more productive and less harmful things, had you not been so impulsive.

Self-control is also very difficult when it comes to responding to our emotions. Humans are emotional beings, so we will experience emotional feelings. As Christians, the world looks at us to see how we respond to various emotions that we develop from certain stimuli. When it comes to spirituality, we must be cautious and considerate, and we must refrain from allowing our emotions to get the best of us. Beloved, don't engage in spoil behavior, having a spiritual and emotional tantrum when you don't get your way in life. When this happens, you react within the tantrum, which means your decision-making is tantrum-produced. For example, my son once had a tantrum because he couldn't get his way. While in the tantrum, he threw a toy, breaking it. Throwing the toy was a decision that was tantrum-produced, but once the tantrum was finished (and I mean quickly), the toy was still broken. Develop self-control by being careful of how you allow situations to dictate how you respond to God.

Aisle 2: Bread Section
John 6:51

Give us this day our daily bread … many of us learned to recite this phrase in our childhood while learning the Lord's Prayer. I used to make fun of the old deacons when I was a child when they would sing the hymn, "Guide Me Oh thou Great Jehovah." When they got to the verse, "Bread of heaven, Bread of heaven, feed me til' I want no more," it never made sense to me. How can bread feed someone? But as the old folk say, KEEP LIVING! I came to understand that this bread that is doing the feeding that the deacons were referring to is Jesus Christ! Look at what Jesus says to the multitude:

"I am the living bread which came down from heaven. If anyone eats of this bread, he will live forever; and the bread that I shall give is My flesh, which I shall give for the life of the world"
John 6:51
NKJV

Whether you like wheat bread, white bread, toasted bread, flat bread, or crazy bread, you know that if you eat enough of it, you will be too full to eat much of anything else. When I was in high school, my teammates and I used to go out to eat after every Friday night game, and we would come up with different challenges. On one particular night, someone came up with the challenge to eat one slice of bread in less than one minute. The rules were, you couldn't drink anything with it, and you had to chew it. I, being the competitor that I am, was definitely up for the challenge after watching other people fail at it. I knew I could do it. I was playing out all kinds of scenarios in my head while being an observer. Well, to save you all the suspense, I lost. The fact is, no one won! Bread is definitely time-consuming and filling when you chew it. In other words, when you take time to process it by breaking it into pieces with your teeth and swallowing it, your hunger drive is being satisfied. Have you ever eaten at Red Lobster or Olive Garden and experienced the joys of their delicious bread? You know if you eat too much bread, you won't have room for much else that you ordered? In other words, bread is filling, and now in my adulthood, I understand what that old deacon was "hollering" about.

Jesus makes it very plain to the multitude that if anyone comes to Him, they shall never hunger. He is indeed the bread of life. It doesn't matter where you are in your life. It doesn't matter which path you decided to take. When you seek Jesus, He will fill you like bread! You shall live and not die. What the enemy has done, however, is to make the packaging or the wrapping paper of junk food look way more attractive than bread packaging, and he has distracted some from even walking down the bread aisle. Can I tell you that Jesus wasn't worried about how He looked. He was concerned about how He made others look, healing the sick and giving sight to the blind. He said in John 10:10 that He's come that we may have life more abundantly. You may need to stop reading right now and check your daily diet. How much bread are you eating? There was a season in my life where I tried a more healthy diet. Instead of eating out at places like Burger King or McDonalds, I'd go to Subway daily. The crazy thing was, however, the more I ate Subway, the more weight I gained. It was because of all that bread! The more bread you eat, the fuller you'll be.

Beloved, Christ should be our daily bread. Grab a slice before you leave the house for work in the morning! Eat a slice on your lunch break! Grab another for dinner! Purchase the loaves that will prolong your living. Christ is the living bread.

"Whoever eats My flesh and drinks My blood has eternal life, and I will raise him up in the last day.
John 6:54
NKJV

The bread of heaven is *healthy* and *helpful*. The more bread you eat in a diet form (not all at once), the healthier you'll be! Eating bread labeled "whole-grain" provides minerals and vitamins to the body, making it a healthy food item. When you eat things that are healthy, it is helpful for your daily functioning. However, when an individual indulges in plate after plate of crazy bread along with pizza sauce, it's not so healthy and therefore not so helpful to daily functioning. The less Jesus we have in our lives, the less healthy we are spiritually and the less helpful we are to our spiritual functioning. We won't possess the spiritual minerals and vitamins that we need to fight off any spiritual health risks to which that we have been exposed. There's no good sandwich without some bread!

Aisle 3: Dairy Products
1 Peter 2:2

As we continue our shopping spree, let's not walk past the dairy section. You'll find the cooler stocked with regular, chocolate, or strawberry milk is exactly what you'll need to put in your basket. Why? The Apostle Peter makes very plain in his address in 1 Peter:

As newborn babes, desire the pure milk of the word, that you may grow thereby,
1 Peter 2:2
NKJV

During my childhood I loved to watch WWF wrestling! My favorite wrestlers were Hulk Hogan and Brett "the Hitman" Hart. I wanted to look just like them. I can remember my parents telling me that drinking milk would give me muscles. At the time I didn't understand. I loved cereal and figured I was getting enough milk intake. No one could convince me that I'd get stronger by drinking it. However, I came to realize later that milk provided calcium for my body. I don't think my family was the only family stressing the importance of drinking milk. Several years later, Goodby Silverstein & Partners (an advertising agency in California in 1993) originated the slogan "Got Milk?" to promote its importance. The ads on TV and in the magazines showed the public that their favorite celebrities drink milk, proven by the milk mustache and a head-shot of each mega star. This ad campaign was very intriguing. However, I realized something several years later. The celebrities' pictures boasting a milk mustache weren't only to attract fans of the celebrities, but also to point out that milk was a contributing factor for their growth and success in reaching their level of stardom. Beloved, might I suggest that the milk of the word has the same implications of physical milk.

If Christianity is new to you, then I know that you are anxious to learn about the word of God. Just as newborn babies desire milk because of their intolerance to whole food, as a Christian so should your desire be with the Word of God. Babies are reared drinking milk, then baby food, then table food. They can't digest what adults can at the rate they can. Don't let the enemy distract you with junk food or any food that you aren't ready to chew. You'll end up falling short of your purpose in life by getting choked up. Even a Major League Baseball player most likely had to start in the Minor League first. Too many times I've seen newborns in Christ embracing Christianity at a much faster rate than they can handle, and at the first growing pain, they weren't able to handle the test because they didn't consider that the milk would strengthen them. Most of us can attest that if it had not been for the pure milk of the word, we wouldn't know where we'd be. As I stated earlier, the "Got Milk?" ad is communicating that milk was responsible for the celebrity reaching their level of stardom. Beloved, it holds true for the milk of the word of God. Through every trial and test, if it had not been for knowing that God will supply all of your needs (Philippians 4:19), your loved ones may be holding memorial services for you. It is by the teachings of Christ and the word of God that we all will grow in strength and maturation in this Christian journey. So, before you rush off into the deep teachings of philosophers and theologians, I have a question for you … "Got Milk?" Feel free to grab as many gallons as you need!

Water Cooler
John 4:13-14

Just over here along the back wall, we have our water cooler. Water is the main ingredient in nearly every thirst quenching beverage. Water is so important to the world, that without it, there is no life! This is what Jesus was implying to the Samaritan woman at the well. After Jesus asked her for a drink, she responded by indicating they had no business communicating with each other, for she was a Samaritan and Jesus was a Jew. To her surprise, the social segregation was getting ready to be desegregated with water, a substance known to provide growth. However, in this passage of scripture, water breaks down a social barrier, while adding to the kingdom of God. Jesus assured the woman in John 4:13-14 saying,

"Whoever drinks of the water will thirst again, but whoever drinks of the water that I shall give him will never thirst. But the water that I shall give him will become in him a fountain of water springing up into everlasting life."
NKJV

Water is man's best friend after any series of exercise. I can remember running track in high school and the need of having a water cooler on the football field. Water was so important to us athletes; we'd have an instant attitude if the water boy didn't have the water coolers prepared. We'd be extremely frustrated with the maintenance crew if the water fountains were turned off. We'd be disgusted if we went to get a drink and the water pressure was low or its temperature warm. Can you imagine giving 100% on each sprint only to find that the water doesn't replenish you? It can make the environment tense and the contestants uneasy because a need had not been met. We felt like water was the key to our optimal performance. However, it seemed water was only desired when we were fatigued. When we ordered lunch, we bought juice or pop. To this day, I have to force myself to include water in my daily diet. It's not something that I dream about, unless I'm hot, exercising, or preaching. However, water is very instrumental in maintaining my good health. Unfortunately, some have taken this same approach toward the Spirit of God. Some only want to drink from the fountain of living waters when they're tired. They haven't made it a part of their spiritual diet. While it is important for individuals to consume six to eight glasses of water a day, so too is our daily intake of the Spirit of God.

Water is symbolic for the Spirit of God in John 4:10:

Jesus answered and said to her, "If you knew the gift of God, and who it is who says to you, 'Give Me a drink,' you would have asked Him, and He would have given you living water."
NKJV

A S A   P u b l i s h i n g   C o m p a n y

With this fountain of living water within us, we shall never thirst as believers. That's why, here at All-Mart, you can bring your coolers in for unlimited refills. Your shopping spree will be pointless if you fail to fill up your water coolers. You can place all that All-Mart has to offer in your shopping cart, but unless you have the Spirit of God in you, your items are meaningless to the kingdom of God. Put in your heart that you're going to include living water in your daily diet. The more **water** you have in you, the more **waste** will come out of you.

I once did a Science Fair project where I wanted to prove that I could remove a piece of material out of a cup without touching it. I was able to show that by simply adding water to the cup, the material which floated at the surface, rose with the water level. As the water eventually overflowed, the material came out of the cup. The same principal applies in life. If there are some ungodly things in you that you can't control, increase your living water, those things will eventually come flowing out. Take a drink!

Aisle 4: Meat and Produce
2 Timothy 3:16

As you continue to browse through the store, you may already possess several of these items. In case some of you who need to restock your freezers, you'll find that we are approaching the section where some Christians stay away from, spiritual vegetarians so to speak. I'm no nutritionist, but I do know that meat provides protein for the body, and the appropriate portion of consumption can be good for the general diet. I must note that I am in no way casting judgment on vegetarians. However, I am comparing spiritual vegetarians to those Christians or religious people who choose to load their plates with gravy instead of meat. I'm speaking of the meat of the teachings and applications of the scriptures recorded in the Holy Bible. Let's look at what Paul has to say about the scriptures.

(16) All Scripture is given by inspiration of God, and is
profitable for doctrine, for reproof,
for correction, for instruction in righteousness,
(17) that the man of God may be complete, thoroughly
equipped for every good work.
2 Tim 3:16-17 NKJV

The spiritual meat that is recorded in the scriptures is not as popular as other food items. Sometimes you'll find some meat is tough to chew, let alone swallow. It may take longer to chew steak than it does to chew ground beef. For this very reason, people shy away from spiritual meat because it's much tougher to chew on. This is exactly why in some churches you'll observe that there are church members who've been in church for some 20 years and still on the bottle (milk) because they can't handle the meat of the scriptures. Churches have split because they were more attracted to the gravy, but more exposed to the meat. In other words, they were attracted to the fill good teachings of the bible from the Pastor, but he was exposing them to scriptures which challenged morality and condemned sin, which may have been too tough for them to swallow, so they spit it out. Some preachers even choose to deal with the gravy instead of the meat because they are attracted to growth in numbers rather than growth in spirit. Let's face it, we all stand for correction at times, and constructively, it will make us live better if we chew on the words for a while, allowing them to digest.

Looking at Paul's second letter to Timothy in this third chapter, most people don't acknowledge the fact that he begins his statement with "all scripture is given by inspiration of God." In other words, he is merely recording what he has been inspired by God to write. The problem is when you instruct people how to live their life when you are an imperfect being, they skip over that fact that you are merely a vessel being used by God to communicate a message to His people. As a result, people will refuse to digest the meat of the word of God, and over time they will become spiritual vegetarians refusing to apply any scripture to their lives. Reading, studying, and applying the word of God to your life can be a challenge because you have to put your carnal desires in check, and if you're still on "milk," (babe in Christ), you aren't able to do it. But naturally in life, we graduate our infants from milk to table food by the time they're in their terrible two's. Spiritually, the process should be just as natural. Some of the decisions we make in life need to be corrected and reproved according to Christ's doctrine in living righteous. Interestingly, Paul concludes this statement by saying, "that the man of God may be complete, and thoroughly equipped for every good work." If you've made a choice to show disregard for the scriptures of God that require you to complete a self-evaluation of your righteousness, then how are you complete as a person? Some have made poor choices and bad decisions because they simply are trying to figure out who they are, but they're looking for answers in all the wrong places. If you need gas, you don't pull into the drive-thru at McDonalds asking the cashier for 93-Premium Gasoline. The purpose here is not being fulfilled. Get the meat of the Word to grow into a complete person so that you can indeed live on purpose and find your destiny!

Aisle 5: Snacks
You may not get full, but here are some quotes to munch on during your in-between meals.

- Don't hurt yourself trying to figure out what God has already worked out! He's got the blueprint, and Christ is the Chief Cornerstone!
- If you feel like your feet have been swept from beneath you, you can always stand on your talent!
- Don't lose the ingredient that gives you flavor!
- While we live in expectation, we must appreciate maintenance. Thank You Lord, for maintaining me!
- No matter how good the wall looks, there are some beams behind it ... Don't forget those who are supporting you.
- What you've been feeding yourself will eventually manifest. Watch your diet!
- Do your best today so you can retire tonight without any regrets.
- Sometimes reading won't teach you as well as what experience will show you!
- If you're in a tight space, exercise your gift ... God will move the walls back.
- Your DISLOCATION may just be your RELOCATION!
- Don't wait for Jesus to be a hologram. Let the World see Him through you!
- Don't sabotage your purpose with camouflage. Be bold about your business.

ASA Publishing Company

- You may not be able to give much to those who are in pain, but a smile can be life-changing.
- If you're allergic to it, avoid it! Don't test your reaction!
- Don't see the SIGHT, see the SOUL and help somebody!
- The assignment may be on the syllabus, but you may not have enough notes yet to be fully equipped for the work.
- You don't wear a Target uniform if you're employed at Big Lots. Who are you representing with your outfit?
- Your words are a product of your mouth, which is the mediator of your mind.
- What takes days to formulate and build can be destructed and destroyed in a matter of minutes.
- You can't MOVE forward STANDING still!
- God will set you down; man will set you up.
- Don't burn bridges you built to get over "it"!
- You thought it was over, but God has extra innings for you ...
- Everyone has an issue ... don't layer yourself with lies!!!
- Don't be like Hefty and put up with garbage!
- The rest of your life could be based on your next decision!
- The Sun is always out, it's just a matter of how many clouds are blocking its rays from reaching you ... what's in your way of light?

A S A P u b l i s h i n g C o m p a n y

- Doing your thing doesn't mean it's the right thing!
- You cannot be identified as a supporter if you only support what benefits you!
- Be the change you complain about!
- It may not be meant for you to be with someone in this season in your life. God will surround you.
- No matter how good it looks, there still maybe some imperfections that you may not be able to deal with very well. Tread lightly!
- Be careful whom you entertain. People will tell you to watch out while they're watching you and not your back!
- The mirror will never lie to you!
- Be careful what you pray for. Just because you day-dreamed about it doesn't mean it's a vision!
- If you refuse to pass the baton, you'll never win the race. If you attempt to run the relay yourself, you'll be disqualified!
- The devil is mad that Jesus didn't own death, He just borrowed it!
- There will be a time where you have to divide the diameter of your circle!
- What's hurting you now, will help somebody else later.
- Jesus didn't GIVE UP, He GAVE YOU His life...what are you willing to Give?
- They don't like you because they're frustrated trying to figure out how you're doing what they can only day-dream of doing.

- If you're having a bad day, tap yourself on the shoulder and remind yourself that there is SOMEONE WORSE-OFF than you.
- Your next could be your last ... don't move so fast! Proceed with caution!
- To survive and be successful in this day and age, you've got to fight like your back is against the wall.
- Want to know the difference between Church-rearing and BET-rearing? Watch the news! Look out your window!
- Ladies and Gentlemen, just looking neat and clean will take you a long way!!!
- For some people, it's not good to treat your mind like your bed, never made up. Uncertainty can paralyze your purpose.
- Make tonight your last night of worrying about it, and make tomorrow Day 1 of your memorial. With the Word you will resurrect!
- No matter what situation you find yourself in, there is power in the Word!
- Ladies, don't get spent by his spinners. You deserve his undivided attention.
- Brothers, don't be fooled by eye candy! You'll never get full, but you'll get sick of too much!
- The way you live is how people respect you. Don't just give respect, be respectable!
- Pinpoint what you're passionate about and PINCH-out on it ... God will enlarge your territory.

- Just because things Shake Up doesn't mean you'll get Shook Up!
- If you draw attention to yourself, make sure we can see Jesus!
- You're not a movie theatre, stop giving sneak peeks!
- Be careful what you walk into, mess always leaves a trail!
- Don't worry about being Made-Up, be Made-Over!
- Your Misery sometimes solves your Mystery … you find out who you really are!
- Keep your head up, but keep your nose down!
- Fresh thoughts can't surface in an outdated mind!
- Don't miss what Lies ahead because you're Laying behind!
- Don't become numb to a good thing because you're previous situations were too cold!

Aisle 6: Cleaning Supplies
Psalms 24:3-5

All disposable wet wipes are buy one, get one free.

Glancing over to our cleaning supplies, you'll see we have a special on all of our wipes. The reason we have this special offer is because you'll need these the most and we want to be generous to all of our shoppers. Certainly it wouldn't hurt to have several cleaning liquids, brooms, mops, and feather dusters. However, our sales team understands that you can't spray cleaning products on everything. You can't sweep everything. You can't mop everything. You can't vacuum everything. But everything can be wiped!

In the late 1970s, a disposable non-woven towellette was developed. Soon after that, a product that we most commonly use today became available on the market. The baby wipe became popular in the 1990s. Baby wipes are moist pieces of cloth designed to be durable enough for heavy duty cleaning. They're saturated with a mild cleaning solution and are very effective. Also known as wet wipes, they come packed very conveniently for use after eating bar-b-que chicken or Buffalo wings, etc. In other words, you can clean up your mess so that there is no evidence of your past. You should know that the same ideology can be applied in Christianity.

Serving God with a pure heart is about cleaning up the mess of the flesh by declaring to

God, "Lord, wipe me down." It doesn't matter if you were known to be a liar, cheater, fornicator, dope dealer, or prostitute, you can be wiped down! The Apostle Paul says it best in Philippians 3, "Forgetting those things which are behind, and reaching forth unto those things which are, I press toward the mark for the prize of the high calling of God in Christ Jesus." There are some areas in life where you just can't clean with certain items. Is it really logical to vacuum or sweep a small spill at the table? Yes, you may use several cleaning products, but a wipe will get the job done just fine! Areas in our life just need to be wiped down. Let's look at a testimonial:

> Who may ascend into the hill of the LORD? Or who may stand in His holy place?
> He who has clean hands and a pure heart,
> Psalms 24:3-4a
> NKJV

King David here is asking a rhetorical question: who shall be with God? Those going to heaven have to be peculiar people set aside and chosen by God. As servants of the Lord, we're supposed to be different. Many times individuals will put their Christianity on the back bumper of their vehicle of faith while seeking a more popular emblem to grant them social acceptance. You're branded by the blood of Jesus, and there should be no shame in that.

King David had some shortcomings in his life where he had allowed carnal desires to make him just an ordinary person. But he knew that his heart needed to be pure and his hands clean to make him peculiar. The ordinary person is one whose concern is not the purity of his heart or the sanitizing of his hands. A peculiar person accepts his differences and understands the need to be pure. Society advises that we ought to have clean hands. When you walk into medical buildings or schools, free hand sanitizer is posted in hallways and classrooms to promote cleanliness and prevent illnesses. Beloved, it is important on this walk with God that our hands aren't spotted with the pollutions of the world. How can you give God a handclap of praise, when your hands are filled with sin? When you're in fellowship with God, you want your hands to be clean. Anything unclean offends God.

Profoundly, David doesn't conclude his statement with his address on clean hands. He knew it was equally important to address the interior. Beloved, just because you've been made-up doesn't mean you've been made-over. You can clean your hands and make them look good, but your heart hasn't been purified! This is precisely why baby wipes aren't just pieces of paper towel. They have a mild disinfectant that seeps into pores to cleanse and counteract bacteria. The bacteria of sin will spread throughout our emotional, mental, physical, and spiritual selves if we fail to treat it. So what's next for the individual with dirty hands and an unclean heart? Be like David, and ask the Lord to create a clean heart in you and to renew a right spirit within you. God will wipe us down with the Holy Spirit. Its healing power is active on contact, but we must ask God to rub the Holy Spirit throughout our bodies because some sin has become gawky and gooey, needing some additional concentration. When your heart is pure, your hands will be clean, for your hands carryout the thoughts of your mind, and your heart controls your mind!

Aisle 7: Pain Relief
Luke 7:21

And that very hour He cured many of infirmities, afflictions,
and evil spirits;
and to the blind He gave sight.
NKJV

Many times the pain of an abnormality has not yet manifested, and as a result people are led to believe that they don't have any health risks. But when the pain does surface, now what? Over here in this aisle, you'll find many remedies and medications that will relieve you of pain for a few hours. I must share with you that only with time, as the sickness runs its course, will you become well. Medical remedies are available to help you cope with the pain. Pain relievers are self-explanatory. They relieve you of pain for a short while, but you must take multiple dosages to suppress the symptoms of the medical issue. I recommend the usage of medicines. However, I must offer you something that can cure issues that medicine can't touch. Here at All-Mart, we offer you the kind of pain relief that will heal you, deliver you, and restore you free of charge. All you need is a crossing commitment. That crossing commitment is simply crossing paths with Jesus Christ and being committed to His sovereignty. This is what happened in Luke chapter 7:21. Jesus had crossed paths with several people attending a funeral procession.

And when He came near the gate of the city, behold, a dead
man was being carried out,
the only son of his mother; and she was a widow. And a large
crowd from the city was with her.
Luke 7:12
NKJV

Jesus didn't announce His coming, but
when He shows up, it's beneficial to you to get in
His presence. He shows up by way of the Holy Spirit
in us who have surrendered our will to his Lordship
and have believed on Him to be the Holy One, the
Messiah. This woman was a widow and was in the
process of burying her son. The bible does not say
what the young man died of, but I can assure you
that all roads of pain lead to death, whether it be
death in spirit, mind, body, or soul. Friends, we
must understand that *pain is a result of an
abnormality of some sort*. Somewhere, somehow,
something went wrong, and we are left trying to
cope with the pain. This woman's pain was
undoubtedly the death of her son, but the cause of
death surely served as the beginning of her sorrow.
Many people all over the world are hurting and
have been trying to relieve the symptoms of pain,
but they have not considered the abnormality
causing the pain. Some marriages are hurting.
Some dreams are hurting. Some finances are
hurting. Some are physically hurting. Some are
spiritually hurting. Some have gone crazy because
they've failed to address the abnormality, leaving
them emotionally hurt. Where did the health of
that marriage fail? Where did the healthy bank

account fail? Where did the fullness of those ambitions and goals fail? These are questions only you can answer! But even after we've answered them, maybe too much time has passed and the ultimate result of pain has manifested. That is the manifestation of the absence of life. When this is the case, there's only one person to turn to: It's Jesus Christ! Just by crossing paths with Christ, life can be restored.

Let's look what happened to this woman's painful situation:

> 13) When the Lord saw her, He had compassion on her and said to her, "Do not weep."
> 14) Then He came and touched the open coffin, and those who carried *him* stood still.
> And He said to the young man, "Young man, I say to you, arise."
> 15) So he who was dead sat up and began to speak. And He presented him to his mother
> Luke 7:13-14
> NKJV

Often times we find ourselves trying to cope with painful situations. Friends, while God may not move the situation, He will simply change the situation. Notice that although several people were in attendance, Jesus still had people who were not aware of who He was (Luke 7:19). Certainly Christ had the power to wait until the funeral procession was over and to speak a word to the widow or to lay hands on the young man. But Christ took the opportunity to change this woman's situation. Many times we pray to God that He touch us instead of asking Him to touch our situations. Jesus touched the coffin which the dead lies in. Whatever you find yourself wrapped up in, Jesus will touch "it," instead of you. It may not be necessary for us to request transit all the time when weary seasons arise. Christ will change our situation while He gets the glory at the same time. Jesus has the power to take our pain away without taking us away. He touches the coffin and speaks a word to the young man. He tells him to arise! With His spoken word, situations that have died as a result of an abnormality, situations that have open wounds because something went wrong, situations that are painful, can be restored! This medical report of Jesus moved throughout the region, and when John's disciples sought Him for his identity, He healed the pain of those around him. By Jesus changing your situation, it will change the situations of those supporting you in your situation.

This was a miracle of mercy to this woman having been a widow and now losing her only son. Surely we know that it rains on the just and the unjust. But sometimes it seems that when it rains it pours! Crossing paths with Christ will get you relief like no other. Notice the widow's situation is not the only one that gets changed. The young man, who was dead, was now able to rise up out of that which was supporting his death. Whatever situation you find yourself dead in, know that crossing paths with Christ will allow you to come up out of or away from those who are supporting your death. You won't find any malpractice with Dr. Jesus. One comforting thing I can assure you is that none of us would have confidence in any medical attention if it had never worked. Being a patient of His, I would advise that you consider getting in the way of God. All the issues that you have, bring them sincerely to God in prayer, and faithfully wait for your relief. God's timing is the best timing! He's too powerful to be boxed into a four to six hour time frame. Just know that when He shows up, your situation is about to change!

Aisle 8: Media
1 Corinthians 5:6

What you take in will come out! It must!

Next up is our media department! Please do not get lost in the 100 inch flat screens and do not lose your hearing testing our subwoofers. What you are looking at is modern day parenting for some families. Sadly true, but it is becoming clearer that parents are allowing TV's, computers, and iPods to raise their children. And of course those devices only serve as the gateway to child rearing ideas. The fact is, generations are now being raised by reality shows that aren't all that real, videos that are movies (actors and actresses), and music that's becoming more misleading. One thing that is important to consider is that while these shows and music are entertaining, those with the gift of discernment understand what's emotionally, socially, spiritually, and morally appropriate. I admit that I, too, watch reality shows and love to listen to music! However, neither one of the two will take my place as a parent. Furthermore, I have grown spiritually mature enough to know the importance of not exposing my children to certain shows or they'll be misled to think this is how life is supposed to be rather than this is how those people are portraying their life to be.
Paul in his first letter to Corinth says:

Your glorying is not good. Do you know that a little leaven
leavens the whole lump?
Therefore purge out the old leaven, that you may be a new
lump, since you truly are unleavened.
For indeed Christ, our Passover, was sacrificed for us.
1 Corinthians 5:6-7
NKJV

Have you ever had bread go bad on you? This is what Paul is saying, a little yeast on bread poisons the whole loaf. Paul is responding to the immorality being glorified in verses 1 and 2:

It is actually reported that there is sexual immorality among
you,
and such sexual immorality as is not even named among the
Gentiles---that a man had his father's wife!
And you are puffed up, and not rather mourned,
that he who has done this deed might be taken away from
among you.
1 Corinthians 5:1-2
NKJV

Paul encourages the church to purge out the old leaven because Christ paid the price of our freshness when He was sacrificed and crucified at Mt. Calvary. His victory over death gives us victory over death! If we be in Christ, we are new creatures and the old self is passed away (2 Cor. 5:17). Why would we want to flirt with sin? Whether it's music, TV, or the internet, immorality is being mainstreamed. When I think about what these shows and music videos have to offer, I think about Satan's tainted promise of prosperity to

Jesus in Matthew 4. I'm sure he didn't show Jesus some run-down village and terrible landscaping. He showed Jesus his best stuff. Sin is attractive and fun for some. If we as the children of the true living God shy away from screening what we allow to come into our homes by way of TV, Internet, or stereos, then we can't get angry at the manifestations of deviant behavior we are seeing in society today! Being reactive to the several displays of deviant behavior is now pointless if we continue to raise our families this way. We need to be proactive now more than ever. It is almost as if there is a new norm through society. In other words, risky is right, and right is wrong! Please, don't turn your nose up, roll your eyes, and throw this chapter down. Let's consider the neuropsychological process of learning and memory and how they both control and influence behavior.

When someone speaks, the listener is hearing them. The listener then processes what he or she has heard, which we call learning. Learning refers to the process by which experiences change our nervous system and consequently our behavior. Experiences are not "stored." Rather, they change the way we perceive, perform, think, and plan. They do so by physically changing the structure of the nervous system, altering neural circuits that participate in perceiving, performing, thinking, and planning (Carlson, 2007). When we deal with what individuals are exposed to and how they react, we can begin to examine psychologically, stimulus-response learning. Stimulus-response learning has two categories, one being classical conditioning and the other instrumental conditioning.

When I was a child I used to emulate things that I saw on TV. My parents prevented me from watching R-rated movies. Interestingly enough, my son has done the exact same thing that I did. He's taken a liking to the things to which he has been exposed. He's a kid, and that's what kids do. They grow having celebrities as their role models and wanting to do the same thing as them. I wanted to be like Mike (Michael Jordan). Every chance that I got to watch the Bulls (Chicago) play, I'd study his every move, and when I played ball, you'd find me shooting fade-a-ways, wagging my tongue in the air, and kicking a jump-man pose in mid-air! I was presented with a stimulus, and I responded. Because I received a few "oohs" and "ahhs" during my games, I thought I was becoming Mike. I enjoyed the response because I was in an environment where others liked Mike, too! That led me to buying his shoes, buying each color jersey, wearing my wrist band like he did, on his left arm. My behavior had been conditioned instrumentally. Instrumental conditioning involves an association between a response and a stimulus, permitting an organism to adjust its behavior according to the consequences of that behavior. (Carlson, 2007). That is, when a behavior is followed by favorable consequences, the behavior tends to occur more frequently; when it is followed by unfavorable consequences, it tends to occur less frequently (Carlson, 2007). Consider touching a hot stove!

If an individual has been exposed to something moral or immoral, based upon the environment that the individual spends most of his time, he will be conditioned to display the same pattern of behavior because of the environment's reward or punishment of that behavior. In other words, what you take in will come out. Just ask your digestive system! If you constantly surround yourself around smoke, you will smell like smoke. Watching or listening to immoral and devaluing media will cause you to be accepting of such behavior.

In the media department of life, you might choose from all sorts of DVDs or CD's, or all sorts of TV shows or Websites. Some have been catered to fulfill your desires. If you ask your average teen Christians why they listen to "gangsta" rap, they'll tell you they like the "beat." But you should know that there is a variety of Christian Websites, DVDs, and CDs that will fulfill your spiritual desires. With that said, let's go to the gospel section. You'll find all sorts of gospel music for your mood. You'll find traditional gospel, contemporary gospel, contemporary Christian, gospel hip hop, gospel R&B, and even gospel jazz. Let's be honest here for a second. Most Christians, who listen to secular music for a living, will tell you, "Oh it's just music." Well beloved, because of the cognitive process, the lyrics will sink into your mind! If you listen to gangster rap and pop music just for the beats, then you have deprived yourself of some great music in gospel hip hop and R&B. There are some very gifted and talented musicians and producers that work with gospel artists.

Go and head up to our listening station! You can browse artists to meet your Hip Hop and R&B drive. You are able to browse the World Wide Web right from your tablet or computer to search for more artists to meet your musical needs! These artists are putting their hearts on records to help promote the gospel of Jesus Christ! There's no excuse now. There's a genre for everybody. The ball is in your court! What are you going to do with it? It doesn't matter your age. You may not want to be 17 listening to the "traditional" gospel music all day, but there's Gospel music that will speak to your generation! Remember, what you take in will come out. Try some different TV shows for a change, look at some different sites, or dedicate a week to listening to music that will promote the gospel of Jesus Christ and ultimately help you be a better, stronger you! Certainly I'm not requesting you shut yourself out from the real world because the bible teaches us to be in the world but not of the world. Come out of that lifestyle and dismiss that way of thinking, to better yourself. Treat your spirit better by exposing it to the Mediator's message, Jesus Christ! A little leaven, leavens the whole lump! We've been unleavened!

ASA Publishing Company

Aisle 9: Clothing
Men, Women, Boy, Girl, Toddler, Infant
Ephesians 6:13

Therefore, take up the whole armor of God that you may be able to withstand in the evil day, and having done all to stand.

Our clothing department is set up in chronological order so that infant clothing is primary and men/women clothing is more toward the back. This design is not random. It simply reiterates the teachings and customs of our society. We invest in caps, booties, and onesies for our babies to make sure they are covered while being in different environments. As babies are prepped to be fully covered to protect them from illnesses, it seems that moving along the lifespan, people are less covered with clothing. Indeed, Job did say, "naked I came into this world and naked I leave," but he was talking about the act of being born and the state of death. We too often see individuals as they progress into adulthood, wear less clothing, whether it's ladies showing cleavage and thighs, or men showing hamstrings, their pelvis and underwear. It has become popular for Victoria's Secret to be public record, and the fruit in Fruit of the Loom to be exactly that, looming! In other words, the more men and women expose themselves, the more exposure they are bringing to themselves. Satan is being aroused by that exposure, as a man or woman might be aroused by the lack of clothing of the opposite sex. Arousal simply means provocation and stimulation. Friends, when you expose yourself to the enemy, he is provoked and excited to attack you.

Paul telling the church at Ephesus to put on the whole armor of God is a response to his own declaration in verse 12.

> *For we do not wrestle against flesh and blood*
> *but against principalities, against powers, against the rulers*
> *of the darkness of this age,*
> *against spiritual hosts of wickedness in heavenly places.*
> *NKJV*

When believers begin to understand the importance of our warfare and the plan of attack by the enemy, then he or she will consider the importance of being fully clothed as vital. Think about it for a moment. In the middle of January, who would allow their children to go outside and play without a coat on, wearing only shorts and sandals? Who would wear a summer outfit in 12 inches of snow? No one in his right mind would. Common sense and concern for our health have taught us that if we are not covered and bundled up, we certainly will become sick with an illness of some sort. We must take the same precaution protecting our spirituality as we do the flesh. Instead, some have mistakenly treated their spirituality like that woman who wears a mini skirt, a bra, and a fur coat in the middle of January or the man who wears his shirt unbuttoned and sags his pants below his knees at a formal event. It's both unhealthy and inappropriate. Some try to redefine "whole armor" to fit their desires. Satan is waiting (going to and fro, seeking) for you to expose a piece of spirituality so that he may be awakened and provoked to take advantage of your purpose and distract you from your destiny. The only counter to this bold approach by the enemy is to put on the whole armor of God.

Principalities and powers are mighty tools of life that are not physical, but manifested through people. That being said, when darkness is the source of those principalities and powers, look out! We find ourselves standing because the approach is such that if we don't stand, we will fall and be overtaken by those wicked principalities and demonic forces. However, simply placing the total armor on, we position ourselves for success. What is the armor??? I'm not speaking of body armor such as a breastplate, buckler, arrow, or sword. What I'm speaking of is *prayer, praise, and power.* We must put on the full resources that God has made available for us to use in combat.

First, there is "prayer." When you have a prayer life, it's difficult for the enemy to tap your lines because when you call on the name of Jesus, demons tremble! When you have a prayer life, God informs you about what you need to do via the Holy Spirit when engaged in spiritual warfare. Your plan of attack is divine! You're communicating with your commander who can see things coming before you. It's impossible to succeed in warfare without a prayer life. When we're caught off guard by the enemy, having a prayer life will allow regrouping! Have you ever been discombobulated in life, and it wasn't until you sustained a prayer life that things began to become orderly? God orders our steps when we have a prayer life.

Secondly, we must have "praise." The importance of praise as a resource is that it does something threefold! Praise brings out the warrior in God. In Isaiah 42:13, the bible notes that, "The Lord shall go forth like a mighty man; He shall stir up a zeal like a man of war. He shall cry out, yes, shout aloud; He shall prevail against His enemies." The New International Version reads, "with a shout He will raise the battle cry." This simply means, when you praise God, He's preparing to battle for you. Praise also confuses the enemy. It confuses the enemy because even while you've received unpleasant news concerning issues, you're still able to shout and praise God. The enemy can't understand how you're capable of producing such a melody in the middle of mayhem. Lastly, praise empowers the person praising! When you've experienced a move of God when you've dedicated a life of praising God, you feel good about your chances of bouncing back and recovering all that you've lost in the battle.

In addition to prayer and praise, we must have "power." This power is supplied by the word of God. God has not given us the spirit of fear, but of power! The power is in the word. We equip ourselves with the total armor of God by being faithful to His word! Many people have become powerless and have lost battles to the enemy simply because they didn't have enough word. Some situations you found yourself in before may have knocked you down. However, when confronted with those same situations now, because of the power that you have by the word of God, you are able to knock those problems down! Get suited up! You've got a battle to win!

Aisle 10: Building Materials
Nehemiah 1:3

And they said to me, "The survivors who are left from the captivity in the province are there in great distress and reproach. The wall of Jerusalem is also broken down, and its gates are burned with fire."
NKJV

I'm not much of a carpenter in any shape, fashion, or form. However, it doesn't take a specialist to understand that materials are needed to build and secure a structure. From childhood to adulthood, we have all stored our valuables in our living quarters, and we secure them with the lock of a door. Some of us have taken it steps further by putting blinds or curtains on windows just so we might conceal our possessions to any potential enemies. I want you to know that it is just as important to do so with our values in life. We have all been taught values in life, and some of us stray from this teaching. Values and morals go hand-in-hand. Some people have not secured their building structures and have allowed the enemy to come in and steal their values, and as a result, families have lost their morals. When you lose your morals, anything goes! You go with the wind! Upon examining our society in 2012, it seems as if anything goes. Immorality has been socially accepted. Nowhere in the bible does God encourage us to live sinful lives. Adultery, fornication, homosexuality, abuse, lying, and prostitution have been marketed and publicized on television shows. Failing to teach our children about these sins can cause them to grow up thinking they're merely lifestyles. Whether they choose to do them is their decision, but these are sinful desires which God condemns, and we must be sure that we are reconstructing the walls in our life to maintain our morals from a Godly perspective.

Let's consider Nehemiah. He was a descendent of the Jewish population that had been taken captive in Babylon in 586 B.C. Almost a century later Nehemiah comes on the scene and is cupbearer to the Persian ruler, Artaxerxes [ar-tuh-ZERK-sees]. The Bible says that Nehemiah learned of the condition of the returned exiles in Jerusalem in 445 B.C. The Chaldeans burned the walls down in their siege of Judah under King Nebuchadnezzar. We see in the text that now in Jerusalem, with the help of Ezra, the temple was built, the government settled, and there was some reformation. However, the wall of Jerusalem (a defensive barricade) was broken down, the gates were burned, and the people were in distress. This made them easy prey to the enemy. When we look at our society we see churches all over the city, a democracy that gives us freedom of religion and social reformation, but to some, those spiritual and moral walls are missing. Sin destroys the structure for people and takes away their defenses. As we know, Satan is on the prowl seeking those he may steal from, kill, and destroy, therefore making it easy for children of God to suffer. If we are going to protect ourselves, our families, our communities from ruin, we must rebuild the walls! There were gaps in the walls at Jerusalem, and the gates were burned (no boundaries). It was indeed a state of emergency. Beloved, we are engaged in spiritual warfare, and our defense barriers have imploded right before our eyes. We are allowing some of everything to take place. When I was a child my mother used to lecture me about running in and out of the house because the flies would come in the back door where the kitchen was. We know that houseflies are some of the nastiest insects around. They do not discriminate what they choose as a landing pad. Anything from feces to fruit! What my mom was really saying was that I was allowing something contaminating and annoying from the outside environment to come in and taint what we perceive as valuable on the inside. We must rebuild!

Still considering Nehemiah, God's instruction to the leaders of the Old Testament was to speak out to society. Some Christians have gotten lockjaw and only want to deal with matters in church government and not local government. Some things we just shouldn't do! Religion is a choice in homes now. I used to get into arguments (ultimately losing them) with my parents about going to church 3-4 nights a week. Families have gotten away from the rod of correction. We've forgotten that it takes a village to raise a child. However, if the village is chaotic, then the child is also subject to chaos. If the village is confused about who and what they are, the child is also. Media has mainstreamed immorality, and these conditions allow for spiritual poverty which should be the concern for spiritual people. It was certainly a concern for Nehemiah to where he was brought to tears:

> So it was, when I heard these words, that I sat down and
> wept, and mourned for many days;
> Nehemiah 1:4
> NKJV

In order to restore the barriers of righteousness, in order to rebuild our spiritual boundaries, one must be genuinely concerned. Nehemiah doesn't begin to express his concern for the welfare of the people until he weeps. To weep means to communicate intense concern. There are so many people saying what we need to do to take our communities back, but they haven't reached the point of weeping over the ruin. Weeping expresses intensity, and someone who's intensely concerned about an issue is ready for action. The condition of the people hurt him and he solicited others for help to restore, repair, and rebuild the walls. They had an empire state of mind, for Nehemiah says in chapter 4:6 that the people had a mind to work. They realized the importance of rebuilding the walls. But because Nehemiah knew that there would be opposition from the enemy, he had a plan to restore barriers.

> Those who built on the wall, and those who carried burdens, loaded themselves so that with one hand they worked at construction, and with the other held a weapon.
> Nehemiah 4:17 NKJV

Beloved, if we plan to restore the boundaries of righteousness, we should expect opposition, and not always from those whom we suspect. We will have to expect haters and doubters. The work to restore our spiritual barriers won't be easy and may seem impossible, but when you're faced with the impossible, that's God's opportunity to work a miracle. Nehemiah says if you don't want to fight and persevere in restoring the walls for yourself, FIGHT for your families. If future generations are reared without boundaries, there is no restraint on going out-of-bounds. When you're out-of-bounds, you're illegitimate, and in any sport you hold up progress toward your goal because the clock stops! There are too many people out-of-bounds, holding up a great work that needs to be done.

It is vital that we restore, repair, and rebuild the walls of morality because like the walls of Jerusalem we need them for **security, strength,** and **structure.** We must be **secure** when the enemy is going to and fro, seeking whom He may devour. He comes to kill, steal, and destroy and without our security, we're defenseless. We expose ourselves to the enemy (it's like that woman who says her man makes her feel safe). We have exposed ourselves because of our failure to acknowledge that our walls need to be restored. Just like me running in and out of my parents' house as a kid, some have been running in and out of the Kingdom of God, exposing themselves to the world. In Ezra you find that the temple was rebuilt, but in Nehemiah the walls were still ruined. How is it that God would reside in a place with no boundaries? We should be careful to go around saying we're saved, sanctified, and filled with the Holy Spirit, but we have no place of dwelling for God because we have no boundaries.

Walls represent **strength,** and where there's strength, there's power, and where there's power there's authority. Beloved, we are encouraged to be strong in the Lord. Nehemiah says in chapter 8:10 that the joy of the Lord is your strength. When we're strong in the Lord, God is pleased. God will be pleased at our efforts of rebuilding walls and repairing boundaries that have been breached. Those walls will give **structure**. Walls are built with a certain structure. To have structure is to be shaped, constructed. Beloved, structure can represent character, and my question is, what do your neighbors say about your character? Children are growing up with no family structure. The fact is when there are structured homes, there's a structured community, and when a community is structured, there's a structured city, region, etc. We build walls for structure because how can you have a covering with no walls? When you build walls for security, strength, and structure, you use bricks made of stone! Walls cannot be built without a starting point, which is the chief cornerstone, Jesus Christ (the stone which the builders rejected has become the chief cornerstone).

People have gotten lost, linked, and lacerated because of the absence of boundaries. A wall announces a boundary. A wall says to other people, "You can't walk through me, you must go around." A wall is vital to a house! There will be no roof or door without a wall, which means there will be no house. Walls are built around frames and beams, therefore making it possible to construct doors and lay roofs. I moved into a new home a few years ago, and the home came with a shed. The shed appeared to be in decent shape when I was inspecting the home. I noticed that the door had been stripped away from its hinges, and there was a hole in the roof. I thought to myself, these are just minor issues that can be fixed once I take ownership of the property. I'd be able to store my equipment and other boxes in it. Days turned into weeks, and weeks into months, and months into years, and I still hadn't fixed the shed. One night, looking into my backyard from my backdoor, I watched a possum gaze around my yard. The Holy Spirit began to speak to me as the shed was magnified in my peripheral vision. I knew I was supposed to fix the shed, but negligence and laziness shifted the shed down my list of priorities. Shortly after thinking about how careless I'd been in securing the valuables in my shed, I watched the possum walk into my shed. I didn't stay to watch how long it would take to come out, but I knew that now I had a rodent in the shed and some of my boxes and bags would be destroyed because of my lack of securing the shed. Fortunately for me, this was only my shed, but how many people fail to secure their righteousness and morality sheds?

When you fail to secure your shed, you'll expose yourself to the lifestyle of that which creeps into your life. The rodents of immorality will then set up a habitat and it'll be hard for you to rid them of the space they took over unless you force them out and reconstruct boundaries. Sin is fun and immorality is entertaining, but God will give all that is good if you do things His way. If you're looking for love, God has designed it for you. If you're looking for sex, God has designed it for you, get married! If you're looking to have a good time, God has designed it for you. It's up to you to define your enjoyment and not let the enemy and satanic consensus define it for you. We must be sure to repair or rebuild any walls that have been torn down and that they are completed with a door. It is absolutely important that we don't rebuild and repair walls with revolving doors because that simply means our values are exposed to the enemy on a come-and-go basis. An open door approach is not a revolving door. Some things have to be shut out and locked out. You have to simply let the enemy know that he does not have access within your walls of value!

Aisle 11: Gardening Tools/ Lawn Care
Matthew 13:24-26

Have you ever wondered why some weeds show up on your lawn even after you've treated it, or so you thought? You must agree that a beautiful lawn makes a structure look more inviting than one full of weeds and uncut grass. In fact, a few ugly lawns can give an entire neighborhood an eye sore. It is important that we treat our lawn with care! Some will judge you based upon how your lawn is kept. No one plans on having a bad lawn or a bad looking garden, but sometimes they end up that way. Some will be proactive, others will be reactive, and then some will just be inactive! That's simply the difference between the type of cultivated areas we see in life. Let's look at a testimonial about lawn maintenance:

The Kingdom of Heaven is like a man who sowed good seed in his field; but while men slept,
his enemy came and sowed tares among the wheat and went his way.
But when the grain had sprouted and produced a crop, then the tares also appeared.
Matthew 13: 24-26

Tare is referred to as "darnel" or "weed" in other versions of the bible, such as the New International Version (NIV). One definition of a weed is a plant growing wild in a cultivated garden. In other words, a weed is a plant growing where it is not required. The ability of weeds to spread is an obvious problem, and their increasing presence means that they will absorb more mineral nutrients and moisture, fill space, and take light that would otherwise be available to the plants we wish to grow. Maybe you've seen some of these weeds in the church that seemingly have multiplied over the years. They take up space in ministries and much of the Pastor's time, but they're not supposed to be there because they are weeds in a cultivated garden. Garden weeds also act as a reservoir of pests and diseases. Nothing looks more neglected than a garden full of weeds.

Tare bears a close resemblance to wheat until the ear appears, and its seeds are smaller (Youngblood, Bruce, and Harrison, 1995). The ears on the real wheat are so heavy that it makes the entire plant droop downward. However, with tare, the ears are light and they stand up straight. The bible says that when the grain sprouted, the tare appeared. Some of us wonder about others. How did you turn out the way you did? How did you get here? How did I let you in my space, my circle, the church? Well, first we need to understand that because wheat and tare look so similar in their early stages, tare has historically been referred to as fake wheat. Beloved, some people are just that, fake! They look like wheat, talk like wheat (while they are in the garden), but they're not the real deal. Good seeds are those who are Kingdom kids, faithful and obedient to Christ, fruitful, righteous, and obedient to parents by doing the right thing and not the "popular" thing. What we find in this text is that there was certainly a *reason behind the replica*, the *reality of our relationships*, and the *reward for being real*.

The *Reason behind the Replica* (tare) is that the enemy showed up after everyone went to sleep and then they planted the tare. Some may be wondering why didn't the workers wake up or have some security team or system in place just in case the enemy showed up? Well, perhaps they didn't realize the enemy was that close or that they even had an enemy. But, consider asking how the enemy showed up to where you are? If you've been on the battlefield for some time now, you certainly should know that the devil knows his way "to" church and "in" church! He's got imps in the choir, on the usher board, in the kitchen, and even in the pulpit. But you can't stop your enemy, you can only resist him. If Satan tried to tempt Jesus, we certainly can't stop his approach, but we can resist him. Though the enemy is responsible for the planting of the bad seed, there's another reason how he planted them in the field. Matthew records it as "while men slept."

There are different dynamics associated with sleep, and there are mainly three reasons for sleep. First, you've been overly medicated or overworked throughout the day and you're tired. Secondly, it's just that time of day when you're routine is to sleep (overnight). Thirdly, sleep is sometimes unavoidable during inappropriate times due to the lack of adequate rest at night. In other words, you were preoccupied with a distraction the night before, and now you're asleep at work or you're daydreaming. When one daydreams, it distracts from the "now." Even the church can be asleep, busy having concerts and cookouts while the enemy walks right into the garden because no one is standing with righteous resistance. As a result, we have communities and churches full of sleepwalkers, allowing anything to come in the garden to sow seeds of depression, despair, deviance, distraction, or disappointment. Satan comes in our homes and in our churches to deposit demons, and he leaves behind what he can to cause destruction.

We must examine the **reality of our relationships**. As stated before, the ears on the real wheat are so heavy that it makes the entire plant droop downward. It is no mistake that this illustration is provided because God resists the proud, but He will exalt the humble. We should warn those walking around thinking they're all that (they've got the best clothes, best car, and cutest swag, etc.). People do the craziest things to themselves because they are chasing pride. They are screaming, "look at me!" Humble is the way, which is why the wheat droops downward and the tare (weeds) light ears stand up straight. Another difference between the wheat and tare is the wheat will also appear brown when ripe, whereas the darnel plant (tare) is black. The color black represents darkness, having no life. It absorbs all the colors on the spectrum and gives off none. It provides no color; therefore it is darkness. But, God has called us out of darkness into His marvelous light.

The reality is, because wheat and tare look similar in early development, there had to be a season between the sowing and harvesting. Time must have passed from when the enemy sowed bad seed into the man's field. The workers weren't unaware because the two seeds grew similar in their early stages. They weren't able to recognize the weeds among the wheat because they were unaware that the enemy had come into their field and planted bad seed. Beloved, it's important to be proactive and to take preventative measures now in guarding our cultivated areas from the enemy. We are simply unaware of the damage that can be done when it's time for harvesting. It's important to consider, counteract, and control the potential influences on our children. Don't get caught up in the "It's cute!" stage. Everyone goes through a metamorphosis, making it very challenging to correct something that has been matured and planted over the course of the lifespan. I'm convinced that teenagers who talk to their parents any kind of way now, did the same thing when they were small children. Know that the seed that was planted only sprouts to produce what the seed was.

Working in youth ministry is tough! Sometimes I wanted to physically pick and pull every weed that was in the cultivated area because I knew that they were tainting the growth of others. But, with the advice and mentorship of my father, I had to take a step back and let God do the work. That's when I realized that there is a ***reward for being real.***

He said to them, "An enemy has done this." The servants said
to him, "Do you want us to go and gather them up?"
But he said, "No, lest while you gather up the tares, you also
uproot the wheat with them.
Let both grow together until the harvest time, and at the time
of harvest I will say to the reapers,
"First gather together the tares and bind them in bundles to
burn them,
But gather the wheat into my barn."
Matthew 13:28-20
NKJV

It's not our job to pick people we think are a product of the enemy because we may mess up. It's hard to tell the two apart during development. Although the apple doesn't fall far from the tree, it doesn't mean it's the same kind of apple. If we destroy things because of a few people, the good seed will suffer. It's our job to stay conscious in the field, to resist the enemy when he approaches the church. Certainly, at times it seems unfair, but the fake wheat, the tare, the weeds will stick out like a sore thumb when trying times come, when fruit is to be brought forth. While you think you're the only one who notices the tare in your circle, just know that everybody else will notice them, too!

It's amazing to see the grace that God shows in this parable. The owner and the worker were the ones who went to sleep. So while they didn't sow the tare, they didn't prevent the tare, therefore bearing some degree of responsibility. When the servants offered to gather the tare, the owner said to leave it to the reapers. They'll do it during harvest time, and they'll burn it. This is what God is communicating to us. He says not to do anything. He'll take care of your enemies. The tare stands straight up. They block the moisture and sunlight that the wheat (bent over) would normally get. Consider the blockers in your life! You've got to know that God will take care of your blockers; all you have to do is sit back and watch. While your lawn and garden may look out of control right now, don't bother getting on your knees, crawling to pick every weed that doesn't belong. God has some anti-weed methods, and life will be restored to your cultivated space of life. Others will begin to see it as beautiful, admirable! Don't do it yourself, it's too risky! Let go and let God!

Kiosk: Insurance
Psalm 91:1,4

(1) He who dwells in the secret place of the Most High shall abide under the shadow of the Almighty. (4) He shall cover you with His feathers, And under His wings you shall take refuge; His truth shall be your shield and buckler.
NKJV

Over to your right, you'll see our insurance kiosk. The agency that sponsors it is Kingdom Coverage. Most insurance has several different policies such as full coverage or no fault. Well, with Kingdom Coverage, the only package available is full coverage or "yo-fault." In other words, if you don't choose full coverage, then you'll be defaulted to "yo-fault." Yes, it's true, if you're not covered, may God bless you. You know what happens when you fail to provide proof of insurance; it's either dismissal or penalty. Doctors won't see you, and law enforcement will issue you a ticket. You should really look into selecting this coverage from Kingdom Coverage. Most insurance companies offer you several packages where you either have a deductible to pay or a co-pay. Well, here's an incentive: with Kingdom Coverage, you don't have to worry about any deductible or co-pays. The price has already been paid in full by the Calvary Experience Group. Well, now that I've offered you the sales pitch, let's look at the reason you need insurance anyway.

For the most part, insurance is simply a "just in case." You never know when accidents may occur, but just in case they do, your insurance will kick in to cover what you can't handle. Generally speaking, we pay insurance even if we never use it. Beloved, I want to encourage you! Even when you're on the fence about Christ, you ought to get this coverage to be on the safe side. Failing to provide proof of insurance will cause you to be penalized! Let's look at the first consequence, lack of health care.

People struggle with illnesses on a daily basis. Think about how many people could be in better health if they just had some kind of insurance. Consider your spiritual health, how much healthier you'd be if you had access to Dr. Jesus. Unfortunately, in the medical field, even though doctors work to help people live healthy lives, you may not get the best treatment if you're not part of an insurance group. Well, Dr. Jesus wants to see those with or without insurance, but the problem is you have to accept this coverage and you must show proof of insurance. Several individuals are living lives with no spiritual insurance, and when the enemy attacks them, they're not able to stop it. Some people who are not covered by any insurance try and use remedies to fix problems that need fixing by a doctor. If we continue to put bandages on spiritual illnesses, we'll end up prolonging the healing process. Countless people have been wrapped in hurt far too long simply because they don't have insurance. They don't have anyone to turn to in times of trouble. With Kingdom Coverage, you can submit your claims to God the provider. He'll appoint the Holy Ghost to work your situation out for you. The more you wait, the longer you'll be dealing with unnecessary issues that could have been solved much earlier. How many families aren't talking to one another? How many marriages have turned into divorces because of prolonged issues? How many lives have been taken and given away because of prolonged pain? Get insured. Your life is depending on it? If not, there will be some penalties.

There are two types of penalties you may receive if you fail to provide your circumstances with proof of insurance. First, you'll be ticketed, causing you to have a record. Secondly, if you're not insured, the things that have been damaged, destroyed, or missing, won't be replaced. Consider the people or things in your life that have been tainted and not replaced. Some people have never recovered from a loss. When this is the case, you are your largest stumbling block when it comes to pursuing your destiny. There are single parents who could have been married by now but never recovered from what was lost in a previous relationship. People who've lost jobs could have reached a state of comfortable living by now, but they became unmotivated in finding another job. While all the time and energy invested is now history, with Kingdom Coverage, God will reimburse you double for your trouble. Consider Job and all that he lost in a day. Some 41 chapters later, did God not restore what he lost? Sure He did because that's what having insurance is all about. In a day's time, all could be lost, and because this can't be predicted, it's important to be insured.

Damages, destruction, and disappearances are evident. For example, how many times have you seen a car driving on the road with a damaged frame? We can interpret that this vehicle was involved in an accident and that the owner doesn't have the funds or insurance to get it fixed. There are people living their lives in a damaged state simply because they don't have the insurance to repair emotional, mental, spiritual, or even physical collisions. When you've collided with some unwanted emotions, unwanted spirits, or an unwanted mentality, it is vital that you file a claim. Don't allow collisions to forever taint how wonderfully made you are. God made you in His image. Get some insurance, file a claim, and get fixed! The woman with the issue of blood in Mark 5:25 filed a claim to be fixed. She certainly checked other providers, but none would offer coverage because of her record. She suffered from this collision and they couldn't fig her out for 12 years. It wasn't until she pressed her way through the crowd and touched the hem of Jesus' garment that she took full benefit of Kingdom Coverage. She didn't need a social security number. She didn't need a driver's license. She didn't even need a job. All she needed was faith. That's the prerequisite to getting coverage.

Kiosk: Vision
Acts 9:9

As you proceed throughout our megastore you'll see several kiosks with different venders offering special deals on their product. Over here we see STGW Vision, which stands for Seeing Things God's Way. Sometimes in life we just have to face some realities! One of those is that our eyesight will not be as great as it was when we were younger. Some of us reach that point well before others. If you're like me, you've needed assistance with your sight since grade school! Others may never need assistance at all. But, spiritually speaking, we all need to have our vision checked. I'm not talking about covering one eye and trying to read letters on a board. I'm not talking about glancing into a machine and trying to decipher micro- letters. I'm talking about our Godly perspective. Let's look at another testimonial.

And he was three days without sight;
Acts 9:9 NKjV
And Ananias went his way and entered the house; and laying his hands on him he said, "Brother Saul, the Lord Jesus, who appeared to you on the road as you came, has sent me that you may receive your sight and be filled with the Holy Spirit.
Acts 9:17 NKJV

What we have here is the story of the conversion of Saul, better known as the Apostle Paul. Paraphrasing, the story shows Paul to be traveling on the road to Damascus when he was knocked off his beast by a light shone from heaven. There he and Jesus had a conversation on his deeds and his destiny. Beloved, you ought to want to have this conversation with the Spirit of God. Your deeds will truly impact your destiny. Saul, at the time, had been persecuting the Church, and he needed to be put in his place. It is not written in our job description to go around putting folks in their place. I'm a firm believer that God can handle this duty all by Himself. In this account we see some things that will indeed impact vision.

One main reason we visit the eye doctor is because of obstructions of some sort. Just like Paul, most of us aren't aware that we need our spiritual eyes checked, so God will do some things to obstruct our vision. When God wants your attention, he will humble you. From experience, I will tell you that you don't want to be humbled by God. Humble yourself! Paul had a plan for himself, but it wasn't the will of God; therefore, God has to obstruct Paul's pursuit. Try not to let pride override your purpose. God indeed humbled Paul! Paul had a great zeal for Jewish law, and the law had been designed in a way that in order for Israel to survive, the followers of Christ had to be eliminated. However, now Paul realized that the one whom he was persecuting others for, was alive. That fact exposed the weakness of the Jewish law. When he saw Jesus, it changed everything. I can tell you your life will truly change if and when you see Jesus! You won't see Him until the Day of Judgment, but His works are obvious if you've changed your perceptions. Look at yourself in the mirror! That's a work of Christ. Paul saw that persecuting the church was sinful and that the law, instead of warning him of the sinfulness of the road he was traveling, had led him to sin. Paul realized that no longer were you justified with God merely by keeping the law, but by Faith in Jesus Christ.

Beloved, no matter who, what, when, where, why or how long you've been doing things your way, God will anoint you with the same zeal of determination, but according to righteousness to do His work! Sadly, however, what often happens is that some who ran *for the world* won't run *for the word*. Those who ran *for sin* won't run *for the Son. Those who* ran *for the enemy* won't run *from the enemy. Some will* run *for junk and not for Jesus*. Some will listen to their *IPOD instead of OUR GOD*. Some will run their mouth *full of gossip and not gospel.* It is essential that once we begin seeing things God's way, we use the same effort and energy we gave the world! The benefits are undeniable.

While visiting any good doctor, he will provide the patient with instructions and guidelines. Jesus issues Paul some *instructions.*

So he, trembling and astonished, said, "Lord, what do You want me to do?"
Then the Lord said to him, "Arise and go into the city, and you will be told what you must do."
And the men who journeyed with him stood speechless, hearing a voice, but seeing no one.
Acts 9:6-7 NKJV

The first thing we must understand before we begin to walk with God is that we can't let others keep us shackled to our past. Some people who you hang with won't understand your purpose because they don't have the relationship with God. Some Christians have failed to act out on faith because they've let others hold them in their starting blocks. Who's delaying your start? A sprinter in track and field begins the race positioned in the blocks. When the gun sounds, he or she will spring off the blocks and into full stride! This is your season to spring off the starting blocks and run for Jesus in full stride!

Paul immediately went into servitude, saying, "Lord, what do you want me to do?" He didn't talk to his friends or family because he knew they wouldn't understand; they weren't involved in the dialogue with the Lord. They had no relationship. It is natural for people to speak against your walk of faith when they don't have a relationship with Jesus. Beloved, some people have religion, but have no relationship. In other words, some of your own church family will doubt what God has called you to do, but don't be surprised by this! It's a natural response for those who have no connection with Jesus.

God will **obstruct you**, **instruct you**, and **reconstruct you** to get in His will. After Paul's plans had been obstructed and destroyed, he was instructed to be reconstructed. God specializes in getting things rebuilt, renewed, and restored. Paul was blinded, and because he lost his sight, he was given a new perspective on his purpose of living. Vision can be defined as the act or faculty of seeing or the unusual ability of foreseeing what is going to happen. Because it's an unusual ability, it's not a guarantee that you will have vision. However, when you do, you'll be able to benefit from sight! Some people trying to fall into the will of God allow others who are spiritually blind to lead them. People who are spiritually blind will doubt your visions! Beloved, don't worry about when people doubt you; they can't see what you see! Your sight can give you the ability to perceive, judge, or discriminate. Jesus says in Matt 6:22 that the eye is the lamp of the body. If your eyes are good, your whole body will be full of light. But, if your eyes are bad, your whole body will be full of darkness. It's hard to set your eye on Christ when your eye is on carnal influences. Sight gives you vision. Vision comes from the eye, and it is the eye where you focus on good, which will result in the heart being good. The eye allows you to discern good from evil. The eye gives you perspective of your purpose! How are things looking for you?

Check Out

As you proceed to the checkout line, please be sure to provide your bonus savings card. It validates that the items in your basket have already been purchased by Christ's death, burial, and resurrection. I hope and pray that you have selected some things to restore what has expired in your life. Maybe you've lost joy, and as a result lost hope. I hope that you made your way to the fruit section. God is holding you accountable to get the things that you need to restore what you've lost or to add what you've never had in your life. There's no reason to remain hopeless when God has provided us vessels to restore hope to our lives. All you have to do is go and get it. You don't have to jump through hoops, turn flips, or drive across town to get it, either. It's all right here at All-Mart! Be sure you double-check your list before you proceed to the checkout. Everything that's in your basket will go home with you.

While we're only at the check-out line, the shopping spree is not yet successful, not until your shopping bags and groceries have made it into your car and into your home. Far too often people have made the trip to All-Mart and things have gotten lost in the move. Don't let your merchandise get lost in the move. You've invested too much time in filling your basket with the fruits of the spirit, daily bread, gardening materials, building materials, etc. The last thing you want is to have had this time in your life be a total waste. Some may admit that at one point they've positioned themselves to receive Kingdom benefits but allowed circumstances to cause them to lose what they've acquired. God has placed some things on the shelves of life that are just for you. There's a divine purpose for your life, and it will be extremely difficult to reach your destiny without having these things in your basket. The enemy comes to kill, steal, and destroy. But God always protects and provides. Be careful during the transfer! Somebody is waiting to gather up what you've left behind. Are there things that belong to you that others have gathered? That means that the very thing that got lost in the move is in someone else's possession. You've come entirely too far! You've made it through too many storms to leave behind the spiritual merchandise that will line you up with the will of God. With that being said, be cautious during the process of unloading once you get home. Unloading can be a bit difficult. Sometimes it may take several trips to carefully unload your vehicle and bring your items into your residence. Several factors may disturb the unloading process, such as weather or circumstances that require your immediate attention. Be sure you trust those helping you unload. Do not let these factors disrupt the unloading process! The enemy will try and distract you during your final transfer, causing items to become damaged or misplaced. Some things that you need in your life aren't there because they weren't unloaded properly.

Lastly, when you're ready to take the items out of the bag, have your entire household help you. They need to see what you've got! This is your chance to share with them what it takes for you to operate in your purpose. Leave no room for interpretation. The piece of wood is not to make a clubhouse, but to build a wall to prevent the enemy from coming into your space. It's to repair what's been broken in your structure or foundation. Let them know that they're covered under the insurance that you've just selected. Let them know how you see things through your new lenses. Share the testimonials that you heard while at All-Mart, how God can simply change your situation by speaking to it as he did the widow's son. I pray that you've metaphorically traveled with me throughout this superstore of Supernatural merchandise. I pray that you apply the messages throughout these chapters to your life. I pray that you take some time to examine your own spiritual residence and to look at the shelves of your life. Could you use a trip?

References

Carlson, N.R. (2007). *Physiology of Behavior*. 9th edition. Upper Saddle River, NJ. Pearson

Youngblood, R.F., Bruce, F.F., and Harrison, R.K. (1995) *Nelson's New Illustrated Bible Dictionary*. Nashville, Tennessee: Thomas Nelson, Inc.

A S A   P u b l i s h i n g   C o m p a n y